SPACE

Conversations with
Florian Tathagata

220
PUBLISHING

First published 2008

ISBN 978-1-905479-04-7

Published by 220 Publishing
PO Box 220, Harrow, HA3 5SW

Printed by CT Printing, China

Florian Tathagata's website is
www.Tathagata.de

You can contact 220 Publishing at
info@twotwentypublishing.com

TO THAT WHICH INCLUDES ALL

EMBRACE

The space for all the marvellous people who continuously contribute to these books by honest inquiry expands moment by moment. Thank you to every being who is ready to live in genuine freedom and the fire of love.

With all respect, I love and honour my teacher Isaac Shapiro. You inspire me to live in freedom, love and compassion. In your presence everything that wants to be met in consciousness becomes visible and eventually embraced. Thank you in freedom.

Thank you to John Stewart, Stephen Thomas, Ingrid Zimmermann and Julia Zimmermann, who with great attentiveness and precision read the proofs of this book and made valuable comments.

Throughout the last three years the friendship with Jim Whiting, my editor and publisher, has beautifully matured. Thank you for the great editing of the countless recordings that have been compiled in the Being Given Space series with genuine interest, love and understanding.

In particular my gratitude belongs to my future wife Julia for her love, groundedness and strength. On this journey of eight years it is naturally right that we are now holding the meetings and retreats together. Thank you for being with me in freedom and love for truth.

Florian Tathagata Schlosser

INVITATION

If like me you live in a city, you may sometimes have a wish for more space. During the London rush hours, packed into tube carriages or trapped in very slow-moving traffic, such a desire seems almost inevitable. In circumstances like these, thoughts of 'me first' easily take hold. But the desire for more space, in our surroundings or from other people, can arise almost anywhere at any time.

This book, the third in the Being Given Space trilogy, is about the desire for space and where this desire is fulfilled. As with the other two books, it is based on conversations during retreats and public meetings held by Florian Tathagata in various countries. A theme running through it is 'being the space' for whatever is given. While we are embodied, the way to life and freedom – the conversations point out – is grounded in the earth; in being the space for each moment, whatever it contains.

Florian frequently makes the distinction between attention turned outward and attention being inward. It is when attention is pulled outwards – to objects, to what others may think about us, to what we think we lack – that the awareness that is our true nature is overlooked or ignored. When the attention returns home to awareness, there is no 'outside' and the space we have been looking for is seen to be that which contains all. This all-inclusiveness is unfamiliar and oftentimes fearsome territory to the small sense of selfhood we have become identified with, which always wants something to hold on to. Florian shows us these identifications and what lies beyond them.

The life that we think is our life is not our life. Our life is universal, beyond the bounds of form, and our life is eternal, beyond the reach of time. It is in a growing realisation of this truth that the nature of life calls us to live in its grace and bounty. I invite you to accompany me in hearing Florian express what this means in daily life, and how we may discover that the freedom we seek is already available to us as the space life calls us to be.

Jim Whiting
Editor

SUBJECTS OF CONVERSATIONS

Space is where nothing
needs to be other than it is
and everything new begins.

In truth you are that space.

Living as space is being
yourself.

Does the space of awareness exist in a still mind and an open heart?

When the mind is agitated or the heart is closed, do you cease to exist?

No.

No. You are aware of the agitated mind or the closed heart. This awareness is who you are. This space of awareness exists in everything. It contains the mind, the heart and the body, whatever their states may be. Awareness is not a state and is not affected by any state. It is unchanging and in no need of any change.

But don't I need a still mind to be self aware?

Is the mind totally still now?

Not completely.

And you are aware of this, or you would not be able to answer the question. All needs belong to life, not to awareness. When the attention abides in awareness, the changes that life wants can take place naturally. They happen without movement of attention away from yourself and the body. Life, from its own intelligence, gives direction for the means and the nature of change.

I sense a distinction between a still mind and the attention abiding in awareness.

Yes. When you are concerned about thoughts in the mind, the attention has moved from awareness to the mind. This concern is just another thought. A movement of attention away from awareness to any object, including the mind, creates the sense of being someone having something. This sense then gets caught in a loop of trying to solve the thinking it has set in motion by moving from awareness. This activity can only come to rest when the attention returns to its own source.

What about the heart? When the attention is resting in awareness, is the heart automatically open?

When the attention is unmoving, the heart is empty; empty of its judgements, demands and expectations of situations, others and yourself. The heart opens and closes as part of the cycle of life. When the heart is empty, its opening and closing is not your concern.

Sometimes I can really be in the body and present and at other times I cannot.

Have a look where your energy system moves to when you play with the idea of 'sometimes'. The first word you spoke was 'sometimes'.

I hadn't even noticed.

So just see in your own experience how it feels when you habitually move into the idea of 'sometimes' – where is the energy?

In the head.

Yes. 'Sometimes' only exists in the thinking, not in reality. If you believe in the thinking, you are going to experience the past as your reality. It is a self-fulfilling loop. The constant repetition of the past makes us feel and behave like a caged hamster on a hamster wheel. Then when we meet together on a retreat, there is some relief until we go back to the hamster wheel. Now that the energy is more present, how do you experience yourself?

Embodied.

Yes, here in the body. Become more aware of how the nervous system responds when we pick up a thought.

Yes, I can feel something running.

So I am only inviting you to notice what is happening anyway. Honour the recognition of that energetic movement. It is a matter of honouring awareness, honouring the fact that you have already been aware; you just weren't giving attention to it. I am inviting you into your own experience. Immediately I spoke of it there was the same recognition in you as in me. The only difference between us is that I honour that awareness and you were jumping over. The awareness itself is exactly the same. I am not more aware than you are; the only difference is that I honour that awareness absolutely. How does your system respond to this invitation to notice what is happening now?

It is relaxing.

Yes. The 'now' always relaxes. The 'sometimes' always tightens up. There is only one time when you can relax; now.

What about memories?

Let memory be here; let it come home into the moment. Just don't pick it up. Don't move into it; don't jump over it. Even painful memories can be welcomed. If you let them be, they let you be. We have experienced ourselves as being victims of life experience but, when you are space for whatever shows up, you are the cause of experience not the effect or a victim. When you are hard with your pain, how is the pain with you?

Hard.

Yes, it gets harder and harder. But it is because you overlooked the fact that you took the first step. You unconsciously took the first step by not wanting to have the pain. And it is that not wanting that causes it to strengthen. You have looked to others to relieve you of your pain; but if others do it for you, you will again be an effect. You have the key in your hands. All I can do is show you where the key is. The way we are with ourselves and our experience is the first step.

When I find myself going through a difficult time, like now, my habitual reaction is to get to work on the confusion and solve it.

This is a circle of conflict. One of the loops we can get caught up in is the loop of creating confusion and solving it. It comes from wanting to do your best. Then, when it doesn't work as we want, there is a sense of disappointment and frustration. This usually turns to sadness, anger and the drive to do a better job of solving the problem. This way the loop starts again.

My invitation is just to allow that confusion to show up in the space that is available right now. When we begin to see through the loop, we can be confused without needing to solve the confusion. Then you can see what the confusion wants to reveal. If you take the confusion to be a personal affair, it creates a tremendous burden on you to do something about it. Let it fully touch you, but do not take it for yourself.

A pattern repeats because the nervous system is looking for an exit. Just before the loop starts again, there is an exit point. The exit is: it was like it was and it is like it is. By this exit, by being with what is, you can experience the pain that wants to be released from the system and the pattern will no longer need to repeat. Then there is the possibility for something new.

It may help to visualise a clockface. Just before 12 o'clock on the circle is 11.59. This is the instant when you can be with what is in the recognition that the vicious circle of confusion is unsolvable. Hope that it might be is 11.59 and 30 seconds. Without that hope, you would not start a new circle. Mankind has been hoping for 2000 years that things would change, but they are getting worse.

So what is the answer?

The only answer – if you can call it an answer – is not wanting to change anything. Then notice how the energy changes in you. This open up the possibility for real transformation. Everything that happens on the outside can only reflect this.

When you speak about 'loops' I would like to be clear about what you mean and how they operate.

A loop begins with an unconscious movement of attention away from embodiment to the mind; a moving away from resting in the body. There is no need to investigate the cause of any loop beyond this movement, because all loops function in the same way – movement of attention to the mind and away from the body. The same situation that from the perspective of the mind seems like something personal that needs to be solved appears completely differently and impersonal from the perspective of being fully embodied.

When we first become aware of discomfort in the body generated by an emotion that we do not want to feel, there is a habitual movement of attention upwards to the head which generates thinking. If we give the contraction in the body a little gentle and conscious attention, instead of moving to the head to find a way to get rid of it, the attention moves back into the body. It is not a matter of solving the contraction but of letting awareness gently dissolve it. Ideas like 'I have a problem' and questions like 'What is wrong?' just vanish. These ideas are just a waste of energy and time.

In conscious attention the patterns do not have much space to play out. So, from their perspective, awareness is their worst enemy. From the perspective of awareness, however, it is their best friend, for only in awareness can the patterns be liberated from themselves. Every pattern is basically a survival mechanism to keep the system going. It is meant to protect the body from death.

But isn't it usually a fear of death of the personality, rather than the physical body? Isn't it the fear of emotional death, intellectual death; everything we think we are?

No, there is no such thing as a personality.

But if somebody feels that the way they see things — their world view — is threatened, isn't that behind most of the contractions? The physical body is rarely in any real danger.

When core patterns — we can also call them our core beliefs — are touched, every cell in the system makes us believe that if we lose them we will cease to exist. The cells react as though physical death is imminent. It is not fundamentally a psychological or emotional experience; it is a full body experience: 'if I give in now, everything will collapse and I am going to die'. When I say there is no personality, I mean there is no-one dying. The physical reaction is generated by the illusion that it is personal.

The physical sensations that naturally arise when there is imminent danger of physical death seem somehow to have migrated to the mental and emotional bodies, so that if someone feels threatened at the level of opinion or at the level of receiving love, they get the same physical response as if they are threatened with physical death.

Yes.

So is this why we have patterns of which we are unconscious? The physical reaction to real physical danger has to be quicker than the mind; people who have got out of acute danger, or who have helped others to, say 'I didn't have time to think; getting out of danger just happened'. If this mechanism has migrated to protect the mental and emotional bodies, they too are guarded by movements of which we are unconscious.

The ways we think, feel and act are generated only by the organisation and reorganisation of the nervous system running on unconscious beliefs. It is the present organisation of the nervous system that we normally do not pay much attention to. Any reaction is generated by 50 billion cells re-organising themselves from instant to instant according to the environmental impact and our perceptions of it. The cells constantly communi-cate in a network and generate an illusory image that something we are experiencing right now is a real threat.

Although we may not detect the exact pattern or belief straight away, we are already aware of a movement into one the moment we experience any irritation in our relationship with the world, other people, the body or the present moment. If we are genuinely present amidst the movement, being aware that it is nothing other than a move-ment tempting us away from the unveiling of a core pattern or belief, it thereby loses most of its power. In this quality of presence, the pattern lifts from the unconscious into consciousness. Once it is conscious, the pattern can no longer play out in the same way. It is seen and eventually freed from its own looping.

Enlightenment is beyond you. Truth and awareness are impersonal, so are beyond anything you can do.

Love the truth and being with those who love truth.

If you want something to do, practise honouring awareness.

Then, more and more, you will become one with truth and the truth will set you free.

How can I live as space and allow life to just happen? I can't just sit down and expect work to come to me.

No, but inquire into how available your system is. Imagine life is a big job agency and huge provider. Life can only give if you are available for life. If you are preoccupied, the provider cannot provide. Life is constantly looking at where it can give. If you withdraw from life into a small idea of what life is, life cannot give of its abundance.

The more you are available, the more life feels your presence. It is like you have an antenna giving out signals to life: 'I am available'. If you are at a dance, to find a partner you have to stand in the light. If you stand in the dark, you will not be seen. So is your system energetically available for the dance, the abundance of life?

You cannot be half available for life or 90% available. Either you are available or not. When you are available, you do not have to worry about the details. Life chooses you. Life takes you where your needs and life's needs can be met. To be well grounded, feet on the ground and fully embodied, is to be available for life. Begin by being embodied and fully present with each person you meet.

And how does this apply to a relationship?

Once you are that availability, it attracts everything. It is like nectar to the bees. But to be
available is to be available for all of life, in every
shade. To be available for a relationship, you have
to be available for loss and disappointment. To be
secure, you have to be available for insecurity. To
be available for heaven is to be available for hell.
But the more you are available for hell, the less
hell there is.

I am trying to picture what this would look like.

Having a picture of what it would look like is not
being available for life. Life is the unknown. It is
leaving the known and giving yourself to the
unknown. But it is not mystical; it is here, now.
This moment is born of the unknown. It is so
near that we often overlook it and instead see the
known, which is the past. When your feet are on
the ground, you kiss the earth. It does not matter
where on earth your body is; it does not matter
which circumstance the body is in, because it is
always here. So you do not need to know where
life will take you.

Can I explore with you that moment when the system starts to contract?

Have a look at what drives that question; what drives the wanting to explore this.

I want to live my life in truth, and I can see how I open and contract.

So what you see is expansion and contraction. Does awareness change?

No.

That awareness is always present, whether there is expansion or contraction. That awareness is truth. You are that truth. It is not that you live *in* truth, you are living *as* truth, or awareness. Does the contraction change awareness?

No.

Does the expansion change awareness?

No.

So what is there to be changed?

Nothing.

So even if you contract, it does not mean anything. You are aware of the contraction or expansion, being closed or open. These have nothing to do with your being awareness. This is most fundamental, because if we think that when we feel open we are aware, and if we feel closed we are not aware, we think we are wrong when we are feeling closed. We feel we have lost it; but we haven't lost anything. The awareness is still here. I am already truth, no matter how I feel.

Yes, I see that.

So now notice how your nervous system responds to that recognition.

It's a huge relief.

Yes. As awareness – as what you are – be the space for whatever contractions remain. They do not mean anything. They can start to merge with all that is now, and they are no big thing anymore.

In the male principle of existence, the creative force is not moving; it cannot create.

If attention does not move, creation comes to rest. From moment to moment, nothing happens. The play of attention is the dynamic, or female, principle – the creative aspect.

The awareness in which this whole creative play functions, or plays out, is space. Space is the huge welcome, the caring principle, the providing principle. It provides the field in which all of creation happens, and it happens through attention focusing on an object and then widening again, like breathing in and breathing out.

From the perspective of being space, you see the game going on – which is the polarity of male and female. From the perspective of exploring the movement of attention, you are exploring the game of duality taking place in awareness.

You have spoken about the contraction that happens when we want something – we want love, we want to please, or whatever. The contraction happens and the experience is distorted. It explained something for me. If I have ever wanted something I have never been able to be who I am.

So let us explore this mechanism. While we are sitting here and speaking, just sense if there is any relaxation happening. There is a very subtle awareness prior to the speaking, prior to the feeling, prior to the thinking and prior to the senses. This awareness is always present, noticing from moment to moment what is showing up. From the perspective of awareness, how does all this appear?

There is energy where the contraction usually takes place, but it is different.

Without focusing on it, see how it is different. We can look at it from a 'me' point of view and the whole thing becomes narrow in perspective – or we can explore everything from the perspective of being awareness; the space that is prior to everything and has never been anywhere. How is it from that perspective?

It's hard to focus on myself.

I am pleased to hear it. I would say rather that it is impossible to focus on yourself because the focus would again be returning to that old mechanism. This space is without focus. You are that which is prior to the focus. See how the physical system responds to being that – just sense it without looking at it. Let the body sense itself within the space – the awareness – that you are.

I feel energy; I feel excitement almost – and yet the 'I' is everywhere.

Yes, you are set free. The way we imprison ourselves – the sense of being bound – is coming only from the way we look upon ourselves. That narrow focus of attention imprisons the whole system – emotionally, mentally, sensually – the focus of attention determines the prison we are in.

That's exactly how it has been.

The contractions have never been real. They were all self-made – a lot of suffering for nothing, trying to solve a separation from life that has never really existed.

Any time in life there is a liking or a disliking of something, we can no longer be ourselves. Our true nature – awareness – becomes covered by attention on particular objects of awareness.

Whenever we are not present, whenever we are not the space for life as it is, now, we are bound by time and confined by place: there is a looking forward to a better time somewhere else and a feeling of dissatisfaction with the present moment. This dissatisfaction creates a doing on our part to get what we want and we can no longer be what we are.

Can you be with whatever is in this moment? Can you be with it without wanting to change it? Can you be with everything in your life as it is? Your relationship or absence of one? Your job or absence of one? Your physical sensations? Feelings? Your thoughts? To be with whatever is, without wanting to change it, is love. Action arises from this love to meet life as it is. Love does not react to what is, but welcomes it with an intelligence that acts without doing; an intelligence that expresses itself without straining for what it wants.

When a thought or a feeling is picked up, the space of awareness is filled by the past.

Allow the mind to be. Allow it to find rest in you. You are the space for it. It does not have to stop its thinking for you to be the space that you are.

Once you see the mind with love, it is enough for the mind. It just wants to be included in awareness.

It does not need your attention; it is happy that you do not seek to change it.

I find it hard to make choices about the life I want to live.

But you do not have a life that belongs to you. You belong to life. You are life. If I separate myself from life, life becomes something that belongs to 'me' and then it is my job to get the best out of it. This is what happens when the focus of attention is turned outward; when we seek fulfilment outside. Then it seems like there is someone 'here' who has to deal with life 'out there' but this is not so.

See how it is when you allow attention to come home. Without being aware of it, for most people most of the time, the attention is turned outward while they are busy with all kinds of activities. They forget who they are.

Yes, there are so many distractions.

The distractions do not have the power to draw your attention. The distraction comes after you have looked outside, not before. It seems like the power is out there and not here, but this is not true.

But I look outside all the time.

When you look outside – when the attention is turned outward – what is your life about?

Activities, choices.

Yes, basically it's about how to get what you want and how to avoid what you don't want. This comes from the focus of attention being turned outward. When this is not seen, you are driven by trying to manipulate life to get what you want.

The whole creation takes place in you, but you are not involved in the process. In the West – and especially in America – the widespread belief is 'we can do anything; we are the creators of our lives'. These beliefs superimpose the human will onto the natural law in the name of being a creator. God is replaced by the sense of 'me'.

This idea of creating our own life carries a very big price: separation, the root of suffering. And trying to do God's job is very exhausting.

I try to focus inward but I feel caught in the grip of the world.

I know you try. But it doesn't work because it is still you trying to do something.

You still remain in control when you try to focus, and it is that control that needs to go. So let's have a look if there is an easier way. While we are here, notice where the focus of attention is right now. Don't do anything with it, just notice where it is. We can feel it as an energy. Where is that energy?

For example, when you listen to me there are two possibilities. You can do so either actively or passively. If you actively focus, your attention goes out to me and you try to grasp what I am saying. This is the habitual way. Is it possible to allow what I am saying to passively be received by the senses? Let the senses work, let the senses receive, and let the system distinguish what is useful and what is not useful. Then see how this feels in your body.

I feel more in myself.

You feel more of your body; it's much more relaxed. And who is making the choice about what is heard?

I don't know.

It is just a natural distinguishing about what is useful and what isn't. It is not a process of thinking. When the attention is not outward, there is a natural discrimination between what is useful and what is not useful. From that perspective, to whom does this moment – life – belong?

To life.

Yes, it belongs to life. And to whom does this body that just sits here and receives belong?

To life also.

Yes. So how is it if everything can just come to you, so that you can receive everything? The confusion you were talking about regarding choices came from that habitual way of focusing on objects. Life is so abundant that you will always receive more than you can dream of. Getting what you want is not enough. You have to trust life and receive the abundance. If you chase it, you will chase it away. If you live the love that you are, everything will pour into you and the world will share the benefits.

It seems that most of the time, without knowing it, we are being our concepts and beliefs. How do we really be ourselves?

If you see what is not you, you are already yourself. Only you, as who you are, can see who you are not. That question came from who you really are.

A lot of my time has been devoted to seeking.

The energy of seeking is just stress energy or fear energy. Without stress energy there will be no seeking. Meetings and retreats are places where stress energy can be dissolved; the dropping of the identity of being a seeker is a by-product of this. In my experience, the biggest human fear is to be truly seen as who we are. When you are available to be seen, this availability takes away the stress and you can truly be yourself. The energy of seeking is actually a hiding energy. It has given you an identity.

But what remains if I let the identity go? It has been me.

It has not been you; it has been hiding you. When

you see you have been hiding, this is the beginning of being available to be seen. The capacity to hold yourself with your feet on the ground when there is discomfort is increased the more you are available. The stress energy then flows down the body and leaves the nervous system through the feet. You may be amazed how much stress energy is still stored in the system. The body needs to adjust to its release, usually over many years. Then eventually the body allows you to rest in itself as home.

The best company is the
company of people who are
not interested in becoming
anything; only in truth,
only in being themselves.
It is rare that you find
such people.

We are so used to thinking we have something to fix that we walk around with a lot of tension. But we can be in daily life in a different way; be with all its aspects from a different perspective.

We can either try to solve problems in life from the perspective of being tense, driven and identified with all kinds of stuff, or in one moment of letting go begin to be different amidst the same circumstances.

When we are tense we are just reacting to circumstances; we never live as the cause, only as an effect. We never feel as though we are living a free life; we feel under the remote control of hormones, feelings, thoughts, ideas, teachers, partners and so on.

The letting go, the relaxation, is not the end of the journey; it is the beginning. On the outside there may still be some unsolved questions, but who we are is another place from where the journey begins. It is the end of the drama that has been created by contraction and the beginning of being real.

Gentleness seems to be the key to being ourselves.

Yes. Gentleness is the key. True gentleness from within; not a superimposed, claimed gentleness that covers our ugliness and violence. I am aware that you love that gentleness, but let us feel the wild side of you as well. Gentleness does not suppress this wild side; it embraces it.

It is the one thing I have not been gentle with.

Yes, but now you can be wild and gentle at the same time. The little kitten we already know. Now you can be a tiger as well. It is just energetic – there is no need to perform. Just don't worry about feeling unsafe with other people when you let the energy take off. Others who feel unsafe with this wild energy are just not comfortable about welcoming this intensity in themselves, so they try to shut you down, but once the whole universe can see us as we really are we lose any fear. We do not have to claim we are something other than what we are; we do not live in our own prison anymore. And again, I am speaking energetically. You do not necessarily have to act out the wild side; just don't try to make the energy sweeter than it is.

I know that animal feeling, but it seems like there is a gap in between.

Yes, you observe it, and by observing you try to control it. By doing this it is like there is always a supervisor looking at how much you can allow. Then you adjust to suit what you think others might expect of you. You are no longer yourself. Like all of us, you learned this very early in your childhood as a survival strategy. The baby is dependent on others and will naturally adjust to avoid creating a threat to it. So can you see the so-far unconscious pattern that caused you to suppress yourself?

To get love.

Yes, to be loved; to be accepted.

It's a lot of hard work.

Yes, you can never rest because you are never yourself. Trying to get some love by suppressing yourself is one aspect of it, the passive aspect. The coin has two sides. The other side of this coin is manipulation. By acting in a particular way, you know how to manipulate. This is what your nervous system learned in the early months of your life. But what is the huge price for this?

Self-hatred.

Yes, hidden self-hatred. What else? You can see the other effects in all your relationships.

I keep them out.

Because no-one is supposed to see who you really are. You have to keep some distance so that people continue to believe the appearance. What else?

There are so many things — like control, and hollowness — and none of it works anyway.

That's right, but knowing it doesn't work doesn't prevent us from continuing with it. There must be something that hasn't been seen so far that means — even when we know it doesn't work and that we pay a huge price — our nervous system continues to do it. As long as we do not feel the full pain of these habits that we learned, nothing changes. So we have to feel the tremendous pain that is underneath; we have to let the heart break by feeling the pain of what we have done to ourselves and what we have done to the people we love without even being aware of it. Only when this pain is felt does that mechanism naturally – without force – come to peace. This pain is knocking on the door of your heart. We need to see the ugly sides of us, things that we do not like about ourselves and that we have to project onto other people – or deny that they exist at all in anyone. And denying the ugliness is living in a dream world.

It is balanced by a huge awareness of how hard I can be on myself.

Yes, when you leave the dream of all being beauty and goodness, you have to be incredibly hard on the inside because, if you believe that dream, no-one is supposed to ever be ugly, including yourself. To avoid this reality, people drink, go to satsangs, hang out with gurus or become workaholics – whatever – in order not to see themselves.

I'm a huge fake.

Yes, 'I am a huge fake' was the unconscious reality.

Space experiences whatever is in itself. Let life, as it is in this moment, be fully in that space. Let life move freely in you. Instead of looking for freedom in life, let life be free in you.

When you let life be free in you it sets you free. Set free what you consider to be your experience – your thoughts, your feelings, your sensations. They all belong to life. They have never belonged to you.

You are the one that gives freedom to the moment. Life is constantly changing so that one moment we can feel content and the next we experience sadness or fear. Can you just allow this to be? Can you be the space for all changes in experience without wanting to change them?

We do not know how life may want us to find that peace and freedom in ourselves. Some have to go to high security prisons; others suffer serious disease. But nothing has ever troubled you. It was you who gave the experience trouble by not wanting it. Whatever may be troubling you now, ask how much trouble you are giving to it.

What we love the most is to be empty, or to be nothing; the nothing that is the space for everything. What relaxes us the most is when we are nobody – when there is no I-sense.

That natural emptiness is filled up by the habit of taking everything personally. We accumulate experiences like old shoes. We like to collect; but what we love is to be nothing.

To really honour what we truly love is to be nothing and to appreciate this in every moment of life. This invites seeing to be immediate.

For ten years I have had difficulties with my neigh-bours. I have tried reasoning with them but without success.

Then move.

But I thought that everything that appears on the outside has to do with how I am inside.

No. Nothing has to do with you. What you are speaking of is a New Age concept. If you try to investigate the difficulties with your neighbours in a psychological or spiritual way, it will just lead to more and more confusion. The way your neigh-bours are has nothing to do with you. When you believe that it has, you bind yourself to the situation you are in.

But what about projection?

Let us be clear about what projection is and what it is not. Everything that you think you see in another person is projection. If I see you have a problem, for example, and think I see what the problem is about, that is projection.

I see my neighbours as pretty ugly people.

What you see are things about them that you want to change; in trying to reason with them this has been your object. What they do is what they do, and if you are uncomfortable with it, move. When the mind sees reality as it is, life is less complicated. If you want your neighbours to be different from how they are you exclude them from your heart, but including them in your heart is not a promise that they will change; neither does it mean you have to live next door to them. You have been trying to achieve oneness with them by attempting to change them to people you can live with or by discovering what you are doing to create what you see as a problem. 'They are wrong' is projection. 'I am wrong' is introjection. Nobody is wrong. It is as it is. That is oneness. So either you move, or alternatively you find a place in yourself where you say it is as it is, they are as they are, and where you are free of constant complaining.

Be the Best, be the Ultimate, be Brahman.

The best is not the end; it is the beginning. We are not starting with problems and then improving until we reach the best. We start from who we are – awareness – and see what flows from that.

It is a different way to move, and from this perspective life looks very different.

No longer are we moving through life looking for improvement in ourselves or our circumstances, but life moves through us as an ongoing exploration of the love for truth. Instead of solving the worst, we live as the best. The best is where the journey of truth begins.

So I invite you to live as an embrace of being human. That always begins by being willing to experience whatever pain is in your own system without looking for someone else or some thing to take it away. Then you not only know that you are awareness; you live as awareness.

You have said that being and joy do not require any particular circumstances. For me, I saw the mind immediately take this and translate it to mean 'OK, carry on being single'. But you have also said that a committed relationship is essential to meet the deeper parts in us that need to come to the surface.

Of course you can carry on living as a single and you are most welcome to. What I have seen in myself and I have seen in many other people is a tendency when we are alone to experience a certain kind of joy. But this joy is usually limited to oneself. If there is any sense that some thing or somebody could disturb this joy, it is not true joy; not the joy of who you truly are. If there is any sense of irritation with a partner, a friend or the world, it reveals there is something you are not at peace with.

If you can be at peace with whatever threatens your joy, then the joy is no longer personal. The joy is not just for you anymore. You are not here for yourself, you are here for whatever is presented. Otherwise the joy is limited to a particular perspective; a certain routine that feels good to you. And as long as that routine is maintained, you feel some joy.

There is nothing wrong about that, but from the perspective of Love for Truth, irritations and disturbances are an invitation to see where something is not fully embraced. There is a richness, a sweetness, a depth that comes from being in a relationship that I have not experienced with anything else. It can be quite challenging, but it is only a challenge because it shows us things in ourselves that we don't want to see. If we can meet these things, the challenge becomes quite easy. What is a problem today can be blissful tomorrow because we give it peace.

Why should a relationship be necessary? There is nothing to achieve. You will not speed up any enlightenment by a relationship, nor will you slow it down, because there is nobody there to be enlightened. When I speak like this, I feel you softening.

I sense that you are seeing relationship as an enrichment of life rather than as a means to improve or become more enlightened.

You have removed much of the unease about being single. I had been carrying a belief that I was stunting my growth or causing some big obstacle by not being in a long-term relationship. And I can see that that belief was making it a big thing, when it does not need to be.

That's right. With that belief, whenever you meet someone of the opposite sex they will always feel that they are a means in your life to your self-improvement, and this is most painful. Sooner or later they will withdraw because you are not meeting them but using them as a means. A relationship is not meant to have the purpose of self-improvement. Many seekers have relationships that are like a permanent self-development workshop, but relationship is an art not a science. It requires a love for truth, but also ordinariness and simplicity.

I don't have anything in particular to ask. I came because I wanted to explore being with myself in front of others and noticing waves of fear, allowing them to pass and finding what remains after each wave.

This is a beautiful exploration. It does not need words, but a question you can ask yourself in this exploration is 'How available am I to be met?'. How much does your system allow others to see you; all of you? Most of us are afraid of discomfort, so we do all we can to keep it away. Can you be transparent? Can life have you – all of you – whether it feels good or not? Are you available to be taken by and used by life? Do you give life the permission to do everything with you that it wants, including throwing you into the most uncomfortable situations? Is this allowed? Or would you prefer to leave now? When people hear those questions they usually think it is a good time to go. Those questions are truly spiritual, because they bring us into contact with reality.

Dreaming of reality or having a concept of reality is very different from allowing reality to take you. Reality is another word for life. There we find unconscious patterns in our nervous system – how we have used spiritual concepts and teachings to keep in control. It is a trap to believe that if we are not feeling good, there is something wrong with us; that we are off track or have lost truth. This is not true. There is still awareness, the unchanging awareness that is aware of comfort and discomfort.

The problem seems to be in believing that I am uncomfortable, rather than simply being aware of the discomfort.

The problem is believing that the discomfort says something about you. Because even if you know that the discomfort isn't who you are, it doesn't change anything. Your system will just use this concept to try to get rid of it. A little gap will be created, a little movement away from the reality of the moment. Simply allow life to experience discomfort in your system. Anything else keeps the sense of 'me' alive, the sense that you are still in control.

How often have you
walked in the park
and not seen the roses
because you were
concerned with yourself?

It is not that you do wrong.
Something plays out in
your system that you have
not yet met. You move from
something that your system
is not ready to feel.

See if it can be invited home.

When you have a sense of space and rest, check to see how much your partner and other people are included in that. It could be that there is just a little more space within the framework of 'you'. It's wider, it feels better, but there is still a framework. It is not living as that unlimited space in which everything can come to rest and in which you are fully available for life.

There is nothing to be changed. It is just being space for others – in particular anyone you think interferes with your peace. Invite that person into you. It is not a matter of doing anything, but being the space for them within peace. Then you live as peace. The peace that is not a full embrace is not peace.

I feel there is now no source to do things from. This is stressing me because it is totally new. It is like I am losing myself.

Who is losing whom? There are many subtle movements that we tend to jump over; so we need to be very vigilant. Otherwise the tendency that is in us to pick things up sneaks in through the back door.

We have to leave every point of reference in us behind. The way you have described it tells me you still have a point of reference where you see yourself as an object. That point of reference will do everything it can to survive. Your view may be much bigger, but it is still within the framework of you. You were living in a one-room apartment; now you are living in a four-room apartment. You have more space, but it is still an apartment.

Gently let go – if you can – of the reference point, which is wanting to understand what is going on. We love the idea that we can discover what is going on because it gives us the false belief that we can control it. The self-observation keeps the 'me' alive. Can you be here with me, letting everything be and letting life do the job?

Completely lose interest in questions like 'Is this it?' and 'Am I doing it right?'. Asking questions like these is a very self-centred activity.

Now I feel you relax, and you are so much more vivid. The way you were speaking before was very soft, but it felt controlled. Now you can be much more free.

There is nothing to do.

Now go back into life and live it until you see that there is no-one there who lives it. Once seeking is over, you go back into life and start anew.

The 'I sense' does not have the power to fool you now. It is still there, but it is not controlling you. When someone calls you by name you will respond. You cannot transcend yourself, you can only be at peace with yourself. Then you cease to be an object. You – as something separated from life – disappear. It is very real and normal and ordinary. There is no special taste to it. You cannot ever say 'I've got it' because that brings you back into the frame. The American Indians say 'If the horse is dead, get off'. All your past experiences, however beautiful, are dead horses.

*I like to have a holiday from real life once in a while.
I like to space out, take a break.*

Do you believe that this trance, this spacing out,
will really give you a break? You are not at your
mother's breast being comforted. You don't need
this anymore.

Awareness is not interested in this kind of holiday.
You may be, but awareness isn't. Awareness is
always on holiday because it doesn't do anything.
As a man you are here to never need a holiday:
you are here to be uninterrupted consciousness;
consciousness without a break for the rest of
your life. Then it isn't you having a rest from life,
but life having a rest from you.

(Laughter from everybody)

We men used to be hunters and warriors, so we
had to go out and shoot deer for the family. And
as a warrior it is good to be awake, otherwise you
get killed. Sometimes the warrior would return
home and lie down on the lap of the woman.
When you lay down your head, never forget you
are a warrior. You don't need women to comfort
you any more.

Do you know the Bhagavad Gita? It is a famous epic of the king's son, Arjuna, who was a warrior and who has a conversation with the Lord Krishna. Arjuna's job was killing hundreds of people on the battlefield. One day he gets tired of this and begins complaining to Krishna: 'I want no longer to be a warrior. I am tired of killing people. Please give me spiritual advice'. Lord Krishna compassionately replies: 'Go back to the battlefield and continue to kill, because this is your destiny as a warrior until you realise there is no-one killing anybody and no-one to be killed'.

When my journey began, someone told me that story. I wanted to hug and love, but I did not want to destroy. Yet I was forced to go back again and again to the 'battlefield of life' until I could see that no-one was doing anything. This destroyed every sense of doership in me. So it is not a matter of looking for an end to the battle, but of realising that neither the battle nor the warrior exist in reality.

In our culture many men became artificially soft. The art of being a warrior has been mostly forgotten; they want a soft life. So for you there is no break, until you see that you are always on holiday; until you have destroyed all that blocks this vision. Is your system available for whatever life brings, without interruption, without break?

Does this relate to my relationship with women?

That non-doing awareness in man is the invitation for woman to drop into her body and feel her body from the inside out. Unmoving awareness penetrates the system of the female and when you meet a woman who is interested in this, and has a matured sensitivity, then her system will start to resonate with this awareness. There will be absolutely no sense of doing in this. If there is, it is not pure awareness.

In the Indian tradition it is symbolised by the god Shiva, representing uninterrupted, ever-resting awareness, and the goddess Shakti, the dynamic aspect of life who sits on Shiva's lap and makes him move. When men live as an embodiment of awareness, the female and male principles can finally meet as one.

When I speak of being gentle, I am speaking of inward gentleness, not a wishy-washy softness that is on the surface. I am speaking about meeting our own sensations with utmost gentleness, gently resting amidst this moment whatever it contains.

This gentleness has an effect on the way you feel, but it is not a feeling. It is a way of being that penetrates the emotions and the way the mind functions. It is a gentle soil, and from that soil grow gentle trees.

We do not have to solve our thinking or play with our emotions. Most people still try to change their thinking or their emotions without being aware of how they are being.

When we recognise the gentleness in us, the thinking, the emotions and the way the body feels change naturally.

People can easily make a 'career' out of seeking. Most 'seeking careers' begin with a big waking up experience that the nervous system cannot hold, followed by a trying to get the experience back. Trying to get it back doesn't work. We become like a donkey with a carrot he can never catch.

While you are waiting for a Big Bang, you miss life. Enlightenment is the recognition that nothing has ever changed. You have always been here.

I still see a subtle tendency in me to want to defend my projections, to say I am standing my ground.

So have a look at what you like to defend.

I want to protect myself from feeling vulnerable.

When that vulnerability is touched, the whole defence system is activated. We are just not used to living with that vulnerability, or nakedness, and we pick up any kind of identity just to protect ourselves.

Yes, I was just starting to do that now.

And once you are aware of it, you are not identified with it anymore. It is enough to see how quickly the whole mechanism shows up and then not move with it. You can make that vulnerability your home. That is where I am home; where I am myself.

We can just have a little drama and we're busy. Even our own pain gives us a sense of security – a sense we are still alive. We think we hate to be empty, to be really true, but the truth is that what we love the most is to be empty.

Identities are very tricky.

Yes, for example I can say to you that you are doing well. If you claim this, you are taking on a projection. In saying this I too can be projecting. I can be feeling a sense of ease in me, which I project onto you and give you an identity of someone doing well. Every time we project something onto another person, we give them an identity – if they want to pick it up.

If you want to speak to someone it seems almost impossible not to project something.

Yes, we have to be very aware. I see so many layers, even with the best intentions. I love to acknowledge people. It feels good, but it can so easily give them an identity.

I can see that acknowledgment was something I was looking for from you, and how I would blow it up – make it bigger.

Yes, that's the game that is played, but we don't have to believe it. If I acknowledge you, it doesn't mean anything. If I don't acknowledge you, it also doesn't mean anything. Human life is constantly getting caught up in interpretations and projections. We need to be so mature in this, and not pick things up. This is my fire too, on a daily basis. Even if we say 'I am nothing', this creates an identity of nothingness. It's a trap that many seekers fall into.

I feel that when I am really present in the body, then there is nothing there and everything is in balance.

Yes, that full embodiment naturally melts all the different identities that exist in potential. Just don't become the 'I am fully embodied identity' though. Claim nothing.

I find focusing on the breath a useful way of dropping into the body. I wonder why you never talk about this.

I agree it is a helpful tool, but I have not so far felt drawn to it because I prefer to keep things simple. My invitation is to meet without a path. Don't watch your breathing; let your breathing be completely free of 'you'. Let it breathe you. Just include the whole body in one instant; you do not need a method for this. Nothing to do; nothing to be observed. Just include your whole system in awareness. We could call this direct recognition without a method.

I am not clear about the distinction between observation and awareness.

Observe my finger moving. If you move with the attention, this is observation. If you just notice that the finger is moving in front of the senses, you do not move with it; that is awareness. Awareness is not involved in the movement. That is the difference between you as an active observer and witnessing awareness.

Do you recommend any techniques?

Most of the techniques I have met in my life have the unconscious message: 'Use me and you will get rid of what you do not want'. But life is not about getting rid of anything. It is about meeting whatever is, from the truth of who we are.

To meet everyone and everything as yourself, gently start meeting every little sensation in your body like a kiss, neither wanting any sensation to go away, nor giving any too much attention. When someone pays too much attention to you, you feel observed and uncomfortable. You lose the feeling of being free. Imagine I am one of the sensations in your body. If you give me too much attention, you bother me. I want to break free, so I bother you. This is the feedback you get from your body when you pay too much attention to certain sensations.

Give the sensations a break and see if they are happier with less attention. The focusing causes a self-centred internal focus. In that, it is not very easy for you to meet other people because you are so concerned with your own stuff. So sense the intensity and quality of attention that your body likes. If you give it too much attention it will contract. If you give too little, you won't feel it.

I have been very stressed recently. It seems to have to do with my pushing things and people away.

That is the origin of all stress — saying no to what is in awareness. Life forces us to take everything in sooner or later. I can hold on to a position in life as long as I have the energy to do so, but as soon as I let go of that position, everything that has been waiting comes in. There is no escape. At the end of life, everything will come home, however much we have been pushing it away. Some call it Judgment Day, but every moment is Judgment Moment.

As soon as this moment — as it is — can have us, stress drops. When things are not working in life the way we want, more than likely there are some positions we have taken, and with them comes a need to protect and defend. This we could call stress.

We have to work harder and harder to defend our positions. Everything that is a threat to those positions creates fear and we see our energy system weaken. The system is not available anymore for relaxation, for immune response, conscious decisions or growth. It is wasted on protecting our positions. The stress never comes from the outside, but from the positions we take. If it isn't a person or a circumstance, it may be some experiences in you that you don't want.

We live in a time of great disintegration. But when you include the other person – your boss, your partner, your kids – the relaxation in your system is available for them also. They can relax in you. Many of us have gone through tremendously painful experiences. We can spend years running from the shadow they leave behind – the fear, the violence in us – because we do not dare to be quiet, turn around and look into the eyes of the tiger; the nightmare.

Once we see the nightmare is in us, we can see that whatever we went through has been the biggest gift of our life. Because once we allow it to be in us – once we allow it to be integrated – it expands the capacity of the system to be present in circumstances we could not have believed it possible to face before. The nightmare we have been through is the real diamond within. I can meet people in their worst nightmare because I recognise it in myself. It is like the alchemy of turning lead into gold. This is the end of stress.

When you feel emotional pain, to whom do you think it belongs? There is a huge confusion around pain. Mostly, when pain shows up we project the cause onto someone or something or introject it onto ourself. When we view pain from a psychological perspective, we try to find its source; but it is no-one's pain. It doesn't belong to anyone.

When relationships fail, it is usually because we believe that the pain is personal pain and that we have to work on it personally. Pain is just something that wants to be seen. In being seen, it can bring more maturity to a relationship.

Problems in a relationship are not a hindrance but an opportunity for something so far undiscovered to be seen. If the pain is suppressed or the person experiencing the pain leaves, the issue is not resolved.

I need some clarity about discernment in relationships. How do I decide whether someone I am dating is right for me or if any discomfort I may feel is just my own stuff?

There is never a right partner. This false idea is a position you have taken up.

So just pick anybody and go?

There is never a right partner. You can search the entire universe and you will never find one. If you can accept this, a lot of stress in you will come to rest. Sooner or later even the most appropriate partner will touch something in you and then the so-called appropriate partner will very quickly become an inappropriate partner to you.

So if I have a partner I stay, come what may?

It is not about staying with a partner, but about staying with yourself. It does not mean that relationships cannot come to an end. It does not mean that you have to stay with a person or a partner for the rest of your life, but we can only know from the heart when it is connected with a deep honouring of the truth and being aware if there is the slightest bit of trying to move away from our own experience. If there is, it is going to catch you up with the next person.

If we do not see that what we are moving away from is our own experience, then it shows up as 'I had better split from my partner'. And the belief is that if I split I will no longer feel any discomfort. But all you are moving away from is the discomfort in your own system. When we cannot stand the discomfort, the whole system projects outwards and we believe in our own projections. You build a bunch of stories around the discomfort, but it is only about something that is touched in you.

When you feel 'Oh, finally I am out of it', more than likely you have moved away from your own sensations, and things are not complete between you. When you have a feeling of guilt about leaving, more than likely things are complete between you.

I thought it was just the opposite.

Most of us do, and that is why people are bound by circumstances. When a child leaves his or her parents he or she feels some sense of guilt. So many people inwardly do not leave their parents, because they do not want to feel that sense of guilt and stay stuck in a sense of childish innocence. They never mature.

I was married for ten years and when I divorced I felt a tremendous freedom.

Wait until the next one. It is just a temporary relief from seeing what is not at rest in you. Leaving, and believing that when you leave you are going to be free, is an illusion. Leaving that breaks the heart – but is true to the heart – brings a feeling of guilt. You have to face this on the path to freedom.

But maybe I just need space for myself?

Many people have picked up a funny psychological concept that they need space. Believing this, they seek to exclude people who 'take their space'. You are space. You do not need space. When you see this, you can include your partner in the space that you are.

When people speak about things being triggered in us, is this the same thing as a negative reaction?

Not necessarily. A trigger is simply something that makes us an effect. It can be something experienced as positive. For example, you are contentedly walking along the pavement and then you see a lovely girl and feel attraction. It's a trigger. It just feels different from a negative reaction, but it is the same. It takes you out of that peace you were in and the whole system reacts to an impulse. There are plenty of triggers that make us feel good, but they still make us an effect.

The negative triggers are a little easier to spot because we usually are more aware of these. The positive triggers are more likely to tempt us into believing they are real. We believe the positive triggers have more value than the negative ones, but we can lose ourselves in both. We become unconscious and live in a split between good and bad.

We have to see how very quickly our system gets involved. There are plenty of things that do not hook your system. What enables you to rest in certain circumstances and not in others?

Isn't it to do with how aware you are in the situation, and whether you have some interest in it?

This is part of it. What draws attention is our interest. If you are a man who is very attracted to women, you will not really see other men. If you love Mercedes cars, you will see them as you walk around every corner, but you will not see other cars. You see only what you love, what you value in life. What you do not value, you hardly see.

If you love truth, and value truth, you are going to see truth in many things. If you value sex you will see many opportunities for getting it. If your interest is money, the same. Start with seeing how limited your focus of attention usually is. From that narrow focus of attention, our life is about this or that, never this *and* that.

Things are always being excluded. We do not live the whole range of human life in balance. We become fanatic or neurotic; very narrow. It causes unhappiness because we are missing something. So can you be here as the space for everything? Can you be an embrace for the totality of existence?

When the space of awareness – which is also the space of enjoyment – is associated with the opposite sex, particular circumstances, particular activities or particular places, the enjoyment that has nothing to do with anything is occupied.

When this space is occupied, we are not available for the enjoyment of everything.

Everything includes the familiar things, but also the unknown.

Are you available for the beauty of the unknown?

I want to do what you do. I want to wake everybody up.

It may seem that I am doing a lot with people, but I am not doing anything with anyone. I am not even waking anybody up. I cannot. My nervous system is doing the job. I cannot control it.

While you are here now, just see if you naturally include more of your body. It is not something you do; it is just natural. Your nervous system automatically resonates with mine and it learns to include the whole body. Your nervous system does the job for you.

A few by-products of that inclusion now show up. You become aware of tensions in the body that you are usually not aware of. The reason you are not aware is that from a superficial point of view they do not feel good. They feel tight. And if we do not want to feel that tightness, the attention moves habitually upwards to the mind and we think. Then we try to deal with all kinds of concepts to get rid of the tension.

Just sensitively allow the body to adjust to that embodiment that is taking place now.

It is a natural letting go of tension; a discharge of stress energy. Have a look how that feels, on all levels – mentally, emotionally and physically.

Mentally, my mind is quieter now.

Now see what is happening at the emotional level. Just notice and don't do anything with it. The 'I sense' bounces off all levels of being, but it is particularly troublesome at the emotional level, where it creates projection. Gently take your hands off yourself. There is nothing for you to do. There is nothing to fix; nothing to think about. You are directly experiencing the actuality of now, in your body. Some parts are more conscious, others are more numb. From honouring what you experience you start to see more precisely.

I am not more aware than you are. I just don't jump over what I am aware of. Be gentle. Jumping over occurs because you go too fast. Just slow down.

My legs are tense. I feel I am blocking myself.

That which feels like a block is your willpower. It is you trying to break through, and this is now the block. What you are discovering now is the capacity in your nervous system to melt its own blockages. Willpower is a fantastic tool, but it is limited.

The block is releasing.

Yes, and there is a capacity to enjoy, a capacity to let this discharge naturally. If you fight for it with your will, you cannot enjoy.

There is now a tingling all over.

Yes, you wake up from that frozen energy in your nervous system. I am not doing this to you and neither are you doing it. Our nervous systems are doing it. I am very happy that you see what is possible. And this is just a beginning.

If you depend on a goal for your happiness or freedom, you are bound by that goal.

When you focus on results, the goal becomes a burden and you become serious. The joy of the moment is lost because your happiness is projected into the future.

There is nothing wrong with a goal, but instead of seeking fulfilment through it, allow the goal to use you to fulfil itself.

If I say I love you, what does that say about you?
Nothing.

What does it say about me if I tell you I love you?
It says I love myself in this moment; I am at peace
with myself.

If I say I don't like you or I don't accept you as
you are, what does that say about you? Nothing.
It says I am not at peace with myself.

Isn't it arrogant to love myself?

Be available to be kissed. Enjoy. Then your beauty can shine through. When you put yourself down, that beauty is not present. When there is nothing to solve, nothing to fix, nothing to change, nothing to be improved, you can be yourself. This realness is what inspires others; this frees them.

I can feel this confidence in myself, but there is also a voice which tells me I am not OK as I am.

So now you have a choice. Either you believe what your mind tells you or you believe in the direct experience of now. Which is more true? What more reflects the reality of this moment?

I feel that, but there is still something that does not want to believe it.

It is just an old habit. It isn't personal; you are not responsible for it; you cannot do anything about it. No-one is to blame; no-one is guilty. It is just an old habit. That's it. Even if you meditate for 35 or 40 years, this will still be there. So you can now relax. The more you fight the thought, the stronger it gets.

My suggestion is a different one. Just give that thought a tiny bit of attention. I see it as a precious gift, because it always gives me a sense of beautiful insecurity. It opens me. If I were 100% secure, it is more than likely that I would stop learning. Questioning enables depths to be revealed in my system that would otherwise remain covered. I have never considered myself 100% complete. This thought keeps me humble. It is a dear friend. So trying to change things is not your job.

This is a big relief.

Now you can relax and soften.

Is sensitivity the fruit of allowing everything to be as it is?

Yes. Normally our attention is focused on what we think. It moves up to the head and we just listen to our own thinking. We then exclude most of the body, we exclude most of the cells, and with that we exclude most of our capacity to feel on a cellular level. Feeling on a cellular level is sensitivity.

The brain is completely without feeling. You can even have brain surgery without anaesthetic because it doesn't feel anything. So whenever you do not feel much, you can have a look to see where your focus of attention is. By allowing the attention to return to the rest of the body – by including all of it – you are taking away energy from thinking; there will be less thinking. Thinking is just stress energy in thought form.

Include the whole body in awareness. This includes starting to be aware of the discomforts, the tensions, the flow of energy – just noticing sensitively what is going on in your system. There is no need for attention to perceive something as being outside. If you let the attention drop all the way through the body and rest there, you perceive the whole world as being inside you. Even when the attention moves out, which it does automatically, don't fly with it.

There is the story of two birds on the branch of a tree. One remains still while the other eats of its fruit. To eat of its fruit is to become involved in the experience and appearance of things. To be still is to let the whole movement of life move freely through you without picking up anything of it. Then we can meet deeper tendencies in us that we usually jump over when we are following the movement of attention.

The 'I sense' always appears in my relationships with others. How is it transcended?

It is not a matter of transcending it. The sense of duality appears in the oneness. The world of duality which exists between two objects emerges from that oneness. It is part of the game. It is funny that people try to transcend the 'I sense'. There is nothing wrong with this sense of I-am-ness because it is appearing as a manifestation in consciousness like everything else is appearing: it comes and goes. Not fighting it is to be the space for it. Sometimes it is there, sometimes it is not there. It is not real; it is just a movement in consciousness. It is part of nature. It is a means of dealing with necessities of life. If I am travelling to a colder country, it will inform me to take some extra clothing. If I need to fly there, it will inform me to earn some extra money for that.

When does this I-amness become a problem?

When you take it for yourself and become it. There is nothing solid there; it is just a movement that arises when needed and can go when it is not. It manifests in different ways. It can manifest as a thought; it can manifest as a contraction; it can manifest as a feeling; it can manifest as a movement. Only when you think that one of its many manifestations is who you are is there a problem. Even if you say 'I am nothing' this is a thought – so watch out. Go beyond the nothingness. Claim nothing, but do not claim 'I am nothing'. Live with empty hands; vulnerable and available for everything. There is nothing to stand on; nothing that will give you any security. This moment is all we have.

Can you say something about sleep?

There is conscious sleep and unconscious sleep. Unconscious sleep is pulling up the blanket and wanting to disappear. Conscious sleep is very different. In conscious sleep you are still available for life even when you are sleeping.

Are you speaking of lucid dreaming?

No, conscious sleeping. When you are sleeping you are aware that you sleep. Even the process of falling asleep is completely conscious.

Does it mean that you are still aware of the body?

No. It means I have so much trust in consciousness that falling asleep happens consciously, knowing that everyone feels me even during sleep because there is no wanting to disappear. The willingness to be available is so large that there is a willingness to be available while the body sleeps. That is what I mean by conscious sleeping. You only need to see how you may be using sleep in order to disappear; to hide from consciousness. If there is any sense of escape or relief from life as you fall asleep, this is unconscious sleep.

Yes, when I get tense during the day I look to sleep to give me a break.

When you do this, you disappear from life. You curl up in bed and sleep unconsciously. When you sleep consciously you need much less sleep.

And the body feels fresh when you wake up?

This is not my concern. What matters is if I am available for life however I may be feeling. You sleep the way you are when awake. If you are not available in the waking state you are also not available in the sleeping state. Sleep is just a continuation of the way you live.

If you get up and walk a few steps, where are you going?

You are not moving.

The awareness of the body here will be the same as the awareness of the body there.

You walk in unmoving awareness, which is you.

It may be unfamiliar to see things this way, but this is the reality.

When an impulse arises in you, look to see if it arises from a sense of peace and rest or whether it comes from not wanting to feel and experience this moment. Freedom in activity comes only from a place of awareness.

You may be astonished about how much 'doing' comes from not wanting to experience what is present.

I would love my family to be with me in what I know to be true.

The question 'How can I invite my family and the people I love to share this with me?' comes from the heart, from love. You are a lover, like me.

There are different ways of love. You can go out to convince people, telling them 'This is really great, you've got to come!'. There is also a very fine kind of love, which more reflects my heart. While you are here now, you can just include your family. Feel them here now, because they are already here. In that, you may not be able to skilfully explain what all this is about, but they will feel that you care and that you start to include them by who you are, not by what you say. It is to live as space – and in that, people will understand what it is about without needing to understand.

What is of interest to them and what will draw their curiosity is how much you live from that place of the heart.

How can I see you and others as myself?

By seeing through your perceptions. I am not over here, outside of you. I am in you. Can you feel me as your own sensations? Seeing me with your eyes is a very limited way of meeting – explore me from the inside. Feel me and everyone as your own sensations. Do you feel me over here or inside yourself?

I feel you inside.

Yes, so we are already closer than close; we are one.

It is common to be so hooked on the senses that we think they provide an accurate perception of reality, but in feeling me inside you, you know much more about me than your senses can tell you. Someone can speak all kinds of beautiful words, but if they are not relaxed inside, you will feel this inside you. You must have experienced people saying things which you know to be untrue or insincere; people who speak about love and happiness when underneath the words there is something else.

Now, where in the body do you feel me in you?

In the pelvic area and in the legs.

Yes, something has relaxed in the lower half of your body. I can feel a shift of energy.

There is less wanting and more expansion. You no longer need to protect yourself. As the sexual energy moves more freely in your body, you can meet others and others can meet you. The separation falls away. It is not about sex. Sexual energy is much bigger than just that. When it flows freely, others are much less likely to want something from you because you are giving of yourself. Everyone loves to be met.

In my work I experience a lot of tension before meeting a client.

When you are preparing yourself for a meeting with a client where is the focus of your attention?

With the client.

But the client is not with you until you meet.

When I am with them, there isn't a problem.

Of course, because they are there with you. If the attention goes to them before the meeting, you are already trying to work out what the meeting will be like; how you think it might be. In trying to work out what is going to happen, you are seeking a form of protection. It is not really about the client; it is about you.

The attention is due to the client when he is with you, not before. When you allow this there will be no fear. A side effect is that you will probably have many more clients. When you rest in that place of gentleness in you there is no room for doubt in yourself or tension.

I embrace everyone, but it does not matter what they think about me or if I am doing well. I used to care a lot about this, but I just stressed myself or tried to change myself to get their approval. When your attention is resting, you do not care what I think about you or what anyone else thinks about you. You see me, you embrace me, but to you it does not matter what I think. Your work will be much more efficient if approached this way.

The only knowing that is of genuine value is that of consciousness exploring the experience of now. When people come into contact with you, they experience that intimacy between consciousness and the present moment in you. This is what draws people. You can only worry and get stressed when attention is drawn away from here.

How can I be free of fear?

Fear may always exist. It exists to be embraced. The fear of intimacy, the fear of rejection, the fear of being seen, the fear of not getting love; there are many ways in which fear manifests. Embrace it as a loving father would embrace his son. Never dream of it going away.

Fear makes you sensitive. If you deny the fear you become like a rock that doesn't feel anything. You are hard with yourself and this keeps you stuck. When you see something in yourself that wants to be met, you see it from a place of punishment. And as long as you are hard with yourself you constantly look outward to get a little approval, a little love. You are hungry for acknowledgment because you do not acknowledge yourself. You have become dependent on acknowledgment from me, from women, from everyone, because you are so very hard on yourself.

I care how you are with yourself. Not because I am a good person but because it is a natural response of my heart. It breaks when I see how hard you are. The hardness makes it difficult for other people to see the love that is in you. So it makes you do so much in order to show people how much love you have. It is a loop.

Can you sense a little softening?

Yes.

This is a very soft process. It is like melting. You cannot do it with willpower. Will has no access to this process. You just allowed that softening to happen. This is what your heart longed for. No understanding can replace it. No concept, no teacher, no teaching. Care about how you are with yourself, not about how others see you. Then you will be more available to be seen by them and the need for acknowledgment will go. It is a process of gentleness.

How is this gentleness developed?

The more awake you are, the more gentle you can be. To be gentle is a conscious decision. Life leads you to this decision. It is not that someone tells you to be gentle or that you use it as another formula or discipline; it comes from your own intelligence, which sees that nothing else can work. When hardness is seen and comes to rest, it turns into compassion. It is the beginning of being yourself. All love flows from this gentle relationship with yourself.

We can be very quick to express our pain and our ugliness. Rarely do we meet people who express absolute love for themselves. Just play with this idea. Explore how your system responds to it. This is an invitation to not hide behind the idea of needing to do, find or be something in order to live as love. Can you be the space to allow your system to come into this availability? Can you invite your nervous system to leave its comfort zone? The comfort zone doesn't really feel good; it is just familiar.

Can you consciously be available? Consciously, not coincidentally. To be coincidentally available is very easy. When things are within our comfort zone we can coincidentally be available. And when you are invited to be, as here, it is also quite easy to be consciously available. Can you let the love that you are, which is currently covered, be completely free; to be available for the whole universe? It is not that it is difficult, it is just very unfamiliar to most of us.

Why do I not want to be available and present?

This is not a good question. You can only notice that that is how it is and then consciously be available. Otherwise you hide behind 'why?'. Even the question 'Who am I?' can be used to hide. 'Who am I? What should I do? How can I do it?'. Here we are speaking about the direct access, the fastest way into presence. The fastest way is 'Here I am'. See how your body responds to this. Does it express greater availability? Otherwise we just believe we are available when in fact we are bound by the known. Explore how much the nervous system can adjust to the unknown. It cannot be forced; it is the gentle fruit of wakefulness.

I'm feeling a bit lost. Some long held opinions and beliefs are now difficult to hold on to.

You are very lucky. An opinion is a refined way of protecting the heart. When you are convinced of your opinion, you cannot fully meet others. You are easily convinced that they are wrong and you are right, or the other way round. So if you enjoy meeting, you are lucky if you can no longer believe in your opinions; the confusion is a very good confusion. It is the confusion of living with empty hands, of not knowing. This not knowing is the beginning of resting in being. Most people are driven to do things because they believe they know the right thing to do to change things for the better, but it is a knowing that is based on personal opinion.

Can I go beyond opinions and be very clear about what is right and wrong?

It is not that you go beyond opinions, because you cannot. See how the movement of opinions plays out in you, without wanting to change them. Wanting to change them is just having an opinion about having opinions. And don't try to transcend them. Many spiritual seekers fall into this trap.

They try to transcend themselves and this very trying keeps the whole mechanism alive. It is a vicious circle. A 'good' part of you tries to transcend the 'bad' part and you get caught up in a play of self-improvement. The mind then believes that if you reach awakening you are going to be perfectly improved. No, definitely no.

The invitation is to gently rest and allow this mechanism of opinion to be. Do not try to transcend your opinions or fight them; you will only be hard on yourself. Have you been doing this?

Yes.

See the play of having opinions without touching it. Do not move against it. Do not pick it up. Everything that comes up just wants to be met by awareness, to be allowed home to your heart. Here, everything turns into peace. If opinions do not trouble us we can sit with our beloved while he or she has opinions and these also can melt away in that gentleness.

Self inquiry does not lead to
an answer we can rely on.
It invites being as sharp
as a razor blade.

It is a constant one-time
decision renewed from
moment to moment;
an ongoing and endless
investigation.

If ever you think
you have got it,
you have not.

Some spiritual teachers say we are already free; others say we have many years — perhaps lifetimes — of work to do before we become free. What do you say?

You are already free. You have always been free. What is not free in you is the attention.

The attention is not free because you believe you have personal choices to make so that life will be to your liking. Stress in your nervous system directs the attention to where you feel safe. This stress generates thinking, which cuts you off from life. When the attention is free, it is free to be directed by life where life needs it to go.

This is the only freedom that is needed; for the attention to have freedom of movement in unmoving awareness.

How is the attention freed from its tendencies to move away from awareness?

By the love of truth revealing what triggers you to move away from yourself and then not moving. It requires constant vigilance but it is a gentle process. Be gentle with what you experience and be gentle with yourself. Awareness is gentle.

Our full human potential is usually not accessible to us, owing to unconscious beliefs and hidden layers of stress in the nervous system.

The invitation of the silent retreats and meetings with Florian and Julia is to recognise that we are not the body, nor the thinking, nor the feelings and sensations that constantly appear and dissolve, but the ever present awareness in which all of life appears.

Based on this ultimate recognition of who we are, we are eventually enabled to explore any unconscious beliefs that cause stress and which determine our way of being in life. This inquiry is neither a method nor a technique nor something we need to do. It originates from genuine interest in truth, a deep understanding of the functioning of the human system and from utilising the enormous sensitivity that we already have.

Silent retreats, mini retreats, workshops and public meetings are held in various parts of the world. For the current programme please visit: www.tathagata.de.

For all the books in this series, as well as CDs and DVDs, please visit: shop.tathagata.de. The books are also available from amazon.co.uk or your local bookseller.